SIMPLE STRATEGIES FOR FINANCIAL SUCCESS

FRANCIS EBENSON

ACKNOWLEDGMENTS

I have always been passionate about personal finance and self improvement. I would like to thank my family and friends for encouraging me to write this book in an effort to reach a wider audience and help many others discover simple strategies for financial success.

Special thanks to my sister Christel Ebenson and Adrienne Thompson for their support throughout this process.

TABLE OF CONTENTS

1 INTRODUCTION

The aim of writing this book is to help as many people as possible get a better handle on their finances. I have learned many lessons in life, from my own experiences and also from assisting others with their journey to financial success. This book covers the major areas in personal finance anyone is likely going to encounter in their lifetime and explains in plain English the things to consider and how to plan and make decisions to ensure financial success and security in the future. This book is intentionally written in a conversational tone because even though I would like to have a one-on-one conversation with everyone, I might not get the chance.

This book will provide you with the foundation and knowledge to better understand your money, make smarter financial decisions and ultimately build wealth. If you are looking for a get rich quick guide, this is not the book for you. However, if you are interested in principles that will help you build wealth over time, let us undertake this journey together and examine some simple strategies for financial success.

I recommend reading this book in chronological order the first time since some principles we shall cover will be referred to in later chapters. You can always return to any particular chapter or section for specific information later on.

Since the majority of us work for an employer for a living, we will start off by discussing how we get paid and the factors that affect how much money we take home. We will have some math along the way but fear not. Even if math is not your forte, you will do just fine. We will go through the steps together.

Now we shall dive into the subject of understanding your paycheck.

2   UNDERSTANDING YOUR PAYCHECK

You get your paycheck and notice that your take home pay is lower than what you anticipated. Why is that? How are these taxes and other deductions calculated? We will look at these later in this chapter. Every employee, full time or part time generally will pay some form of payroll tax such as federal income tax, social security tax, Medicare tax and/or state taxes. In addition, there may be other pretax or after tax deductions taken from your pay such as contributions to retirement accounts, if you signed up for one.

Federal taxes deducted from your pay are calculated as a percentage of your taxable income. Contributions to retirement accounts, health savings accounts and insurance premiums are generally deducted from your income before federal taxes are calculated. Retirement contributions made through payroll deductions to Roth retirement accounts will be taxed.

Only insurance premium deductions are exempt from Medicare and social security taxes. Your net income before contributions to retirement accounts is taxed for Medicare and Social Security. These two taxes are also referred to as FICA, Federal Insurance Contribution Act.

2.1   WHAT IS MY TAXABLE INCOME?

Taxable income is the amount of money earned that is subjected to taxation.
The Internal Revenue Service (IRS) has tables you can use to calculate required federal taxes and we shall use one of those shortly to demonstrate an example of calculating your taxes and net pay. The table from IRS Publication 15 is shown below for the year 2016.

The Medicare tax rate is currently 1.45% each for employer and employees and Social Security is 6.2% for the employee and 6.2% for the employer. Social Security taxes are applied only on income up to $118,500 annually. There is an additional 0.9% Medicare tax levied on any income above $200,000 paid to employees and the self-employed. Refer to the most recent IRS publication 15, Employer's Tax Guide, for any changes in tax rates and income limits.

If you are self-employed, you are responsible for the entire 2.9% (1.45% employee +1.45% employer) Medicare tax plus an additional 0.9% for income in excess of $200,000 and the total 12.4% (6.2% employee + 6.2% employer) of Social Security tax on amounts up to $118,500. Be sure to put aside enough money to cover all of your taxes.

2.1.1 TABLE A: 2016 IRS PUBLICATION 15, TABLE 2. BI-WEEKLY PAY FOR SINGLE PERSON

Not over $87 – Not taxed*

Over*	But not Over*				Of excess over
$87	$443	$0.00	Plus	10%	$87
$443	$1,535	$35.60		15%	$443
$1,535	$3,592	$199.40		25%	$1,535
$3,592	$7,400	$713.65		28%	$3,592
$7,400	$15,985	$1,779.89		33%	$7,400
$15,985		$4,612.94		35%	$15,985

* The amount of wages (after subtracting withholding allowance)

EXAMPLE:
Jane has a 2016 biweekly income of $4,500, is single and claims 1 allowance on her W-4 form. Her additional payroll deductions are as follows:
14% of her pay contributed towards retirement savings in a traditional 401K account
$55 Biweekly medical insurance
$25 biweekly dental insurance
$10 biweekly vision insurance

What is Jane's taxable income (federal tax)?
What is her take home pay if she lives in Texas?
What is her take home pay if she lives in Pennsylvania?

ANSWER:

Taxable income = Gross income - non taxable deductions

To calculate Jane's taxable income, you have to subtract her non taxable deductions which in this case are her insurance payments and contributions to her retirement account. This means Jane is allowed to make these contributions with pretax dollars.

Taxable income = $4,500 - (0.14 x $4,500) - $55 - $25 - $10
              = $3,780

This means of her gross income of $4,500, Jane will have to pay federal taxes on $3,780.

2. If Jane lives in Texas, she will not pay any state income tax. Texas does not charge a state income tax but does have a sales tax associated with each purchase. Jane's taxes in this case will be federal, Medicare (1.45%) and social security (6.2%), all calculated using the IRS tables and her taxable income calculated above. Recall that only insurance premiums deductions are exempt from Medicare and social security taxes.

Take home pay = Taxable income - taxes paid (Medicare, social security, state taxes)

Taxes paid:
Medicare tax = Medicare tax rate x (gross income–medical ins. – dental ins. –vision ins.)
              = 0.0145 x ($4,500 -$55 - $25 - $10) = $63.95

Social security tax = 0.062 x ($4,500 -$55 - $25 - $10) = $273.42

Federal taxes:

Since Jane claims 1 allowance on her W-4, we refer to IRS publication 15; table 5 where the amount of one withholding allowance for an employee getting paid bi-weekly is stated as $155.80

Jane's Withholding allowance amount: $155.80

Federal taxable wages: $3,780 - $155.80 = $3,624.20

Per biweekly pay tax table previously shown, Jane's income is over $3,592 but not over $7,400

Federal taxes = $713.65 + 0.28 x ($3,624.20 - $3,592) = $722.67

Take home pay:

Take home pay = Gross pay – taxes (Federal, social security, Medicare) – other deductions (401K & insurance premiums)

= $4,500 – $722.67 - $273.42 - $63.95 - $630 - $55 - $25 - $10 = **$2,719.96**

3. If Jane lived in Pennsylvania (PA), her take home pay will be the value calculated above, less the 3.07% flat rate tax imposed by the state. State tax is calculated as a percentage of gross income.

PA state tax = 0.0307 x $4,500 = $138.15

PA take home pay = $2,719.96 – $138.15 = **$2,581.81**

2.2 UNDERSTANDING FEDERAL TAX
BRACKETS

Some people incorrectly report their highest (federal) tax bracket as if it was the single tax rate they are assessed. Jane's highest tax bracket in the example is 28%. However, from the federal tax dollar amount we calculated, her effective tax rate is about 20% ($722.67/$3,624.20). This is eight percent less than her maximum tax bracket.

In the bi-weekly pay tax table below (refer to table to easily comprehend this next point), there is a dollar amount of taxes listed in addition to a percentage of income in excess of a specified amount. Income over $87 but not over $443 tax is $0 plus 10% of excess over $87; the $0 accounts for the $0 tax for income not over $87. For income over $443 but not over $1,535, tax is $35.60 plus 15% of excess over $433; the $35.60 is equal to the total tax from the previous brackets ($0 for income bracket under $87 plus $35.60 for income bracket $433 to $1,535). To use this table, simply go to the range that contains your income in the table, use the dollar amount and percentage specified.

For a better understanding of tax brackets and how taxes are calculated, we will calculate the taxes for each bracket Jane's income covers and see how the taxes we calculate relate to the tax table used. Remember from our previous example, Jane's taxable income is $3,624.20

Not over $87 – Not taxed*

Over*	But not Over*				Of excess over
$87	$443	$0.00	Plus	10%	$87
$443	$1,535	$35.60		15%	$443
$1,535	$3,592	$199.40		25%	$1,535

Over*	But not Over*				Of excess over
$3,592	$7,400	$713.65		28%	$3,592
$7,400	$15,985	$1,779.89		33%	$7,400
$15,985		$4,612.94		35%	$15,985

* The amount of wages (after subtracting withholding allowance)

Jane's income falls into five tax brackets, 0%, 10%, 15%, 25% and 28%

Tax Bracket 1

The first $0 to $87 of Jane's wages are **not taxed ($0)**

Tax Bracket 2

Over $87 but less than $443 is taxed at $0 plus 10% of excess over $87

Tax 2 = **$0** + 0.1 x ($443 - $87) = **$35.60**

Tax Bracket 3

Over $443 but under $1,535 is taxed at $35.60 plus 15% over $443

Tax 3 = **$35.60** + 0.15 x ($1,535 - $443) = **$199.40**

Tax Bracket 4

Over $1,535 but under $3,592 is taxed at $199.40 plus 25% over $1,535

Tax 4 = **$199.40** + 0.25 x ($3,592 - $1,535) = **$713.65**

Tax Bracket 5

Over $3,592 but under $7,400 is taxed at $713.65 plus 28% over $3,592; Jane's taxable income (max) is $3,624.20

Tax 5 = **$713.65** + 0.28 x ($3,624.20 - $3,592) = $722.67

If you follow the calculated taxes in bold, it will be clear how the dollar amount for each tax bracket in the previous table came about. The tax dollar amount ($0) calculated for bracket 1 is used in the formula for bracket 2 as a starting dollar amount plus 10 percent of income within the specified range. The same is true for bracket 3, starting with $35.60 (total taxes in bracket 2 + bracket 1) plus 15% of income within a specified range and so on. Even if you earned $250,000 a year, portions of your income are taxed at different rates. You should focus more on understanding your effective federal income tax rate as this is a more meaningful number to know.

In our example above, Jane's effective tax rate = total taxes paid / taxable income

$$= $722.67 / $3624.20 \text{ x } 100\%$$

$$= 20.0\%$$

Even though a portion of Jane's income is taxed at 28%, her effective tax rate is 20%, meaning Jane's taxes will be 20% of her taxable income.

3 BUDGETING AND SAVING

Imagine you have a container with holes of various sizes at the bottom. If this container is under a faucet, as long as the amount of water flowing into the container is greater than the water leaking out, you will accumulate water and eventually fill the container. The rate at which the container is filled can be increased by plugging some of the holes.

Your financial situation is similar to the container above. Water flowing in from the faucet is analogous to your total income from your job and/or investments. The holes at the bottom represent your various expenditures, including financial commitments you have that require you to make periodic payments. If your income is greater than the dollar amount of all your financial commitments, then you can start accumulating savings and building wealth. This is a simple but very accurate example as it is easy to picture in your mind. To build savings and eventually wealth, you need to maximize your sources of income (increase water flow rate into the container) and minimize your expenditures (plug holes in the container). In order to do this, you need to create a budget.

3.1 BUDGETING

A budget is a summary of your estimated income and expenses. Some of the items that can be included in your budget are as follows:

1. Take home pay (after taxes and all payroll deductions)
2. Other income (investments, hobbies etc.)
3. FUTURE
   a. Savings/Investments contribution
   b. College Savings

4. HOME
    a. Mortgage/Rent
    b. Insurance
    c. Homeowners Association (HOA) fees
    d. Alarm monitoring
    e. Home repairs
5. UTILITIES
    a. Electricity
    b. Water
    c. Gas
    d. Cable/TV/Internet/Other subscriptions
    e. Phone
6. CAR/TRANSPORTATION
    a. Car payments
    b. Fuel
    c. Insurance
    d. Repair/Service
    e. Public transportation
    f. Other (Toll, vehicle registration, etc.)
7. FOOD
    a. Groceries
    b. Restaurants
8. FAMILY
    a. Childcare
    b. Diapers
    c. Clothing
    d. After school programs
9. HEALTH
    a. Gym membership or fitness interests
    b. Doctor visits
    c. Medications

10. EDUCATION
    a. Tuition, fees and boarding
    b. Books and Supplies
11. MISCELLANEOUS
    a. Charitable contributions
    b. Entertainment
    c. Travel expenses

Feel free to include additional items applicable to you and not listed above. The dollar amount for each item should be specified next to it. If the sum of all your expenditures exceeds your income, revisit each entry in your budget and consider if you can live without it or decrease the amount allotted to it. The aim again is to ensure that you have income exceeding expenditure.

To properly manage a budget, you should know the difference between needs and wants. Needs are absolute musts that you cannot do without. For example, if you live on your own, you need to pay either rent or a mortgage (unless you want to share your secret on how you legally live for free. Living in a dumpster does not count!). Cable TV service at your home is a want. You will not face any severe hardship if you do not have cable. I know some people will contend cable TV is essential but it still is a want, not a need.

To minimize expenditure and maximize savings/investments, your budget will most likely have to be tweaked occasionally. This is where your understanding and mastery of needs and wants come into play. You can cut out some of your wants in order to save more money. You can also scale down on expenses for your needs such as renting a cheaper and/or smaller apartment or buying a less expensive home. You can shop around for lower insurance premiums, better rates on phone/internet service, etc. All of these can be done but they require a little effort from you. The intent is to minimize your total expenditure as much as possible.

3.2 SAVINGS

Your savings are the positive dollar amount left when your total expenditure is subtracted from your total income. If your expenditure exceeds your income, then there is nothing left for savings.

Set a goal to build savings a safety net that can cover your expenditure for at least 6 months. I personally would recommend saving to meet your needs for a year in case you are unable to work or generate income to cover these expenses due to poor health, layoff or a host of other reasons. This safety net should be different from your emergency funds you plan to use in case you have other unplanned expenses such as car repairs. Find a high yield savings account for your safety net or you could consider buying certificates of deposits (CDs) or some other investment option with low risk that can easily be converted to cash (liquidated). If you have enough savings for a year, consider buying CDs monthly for the amount equivalent to what you would need each month should you lose your primary source of income. If the CDs mature in one year, by the time you are done purchasing the last (12th) CD, the first CD is just about matured. If you let the CDs continuously renew, you will always have a maturing CD every month thereafter which can be liquidated in case you need to cash out to meet monthly expenses. This method may not work for everyone and you should carefully review your financial situation before deciding which option is best for you. Leaving your safety net savings in a savings account maximizes liquidity but the corresponding interest rate may be far below inflation, causing you to lose purchasing power.

In society today, it seems cost savings are praised more than savings. What is the difference? Cost savings are achieved when you pay an amount less than the typical selling price for certain goods or services. Think of when stores advertise sales of 40% off for example. This is a 40% cost savings; the item still costs you money, just 40% less than normal price.

I would like you to slightly change how you view the term savings towards its actual meaning. Let me give an example; John buys a shirt originally $50 but marked down 40% to a final sale price of $30. Does he save $20? This is where I want you to change your view of savings. My answer is NO; John does not save $20. Actually John spent $30 but achieved a cost savings of $20. True savings would have been achieved if John eliminated the expense of buying the shirt all together. Commercials on media (TV, radio, Social…) all push the idea of cost savings as savings but now you know better.

You should set savings goals and divide them into smaller milestones so you are encouraged as these milestones are achieved. For example, if you plan to save $10,000 in one year to add to your emergency fund, instead of just tracking your progress to $10,000, divide your goal into quarters. There are four quarters in a year so dividing $10,000 by 4 gives $2,500. Your smaller milestone is to achieve a savings now of $2,500 every three months (quarter). Even though at the end of the one year period the result is still the same, it is mentally much easier tracking with $2,500 because you get to celebrate small milestones along the journey. The intent to save $2,500 every three months should register to you as a minimum requirement. Whenever you can put a little more away, do not hesitate to do so.

I will not go into details about investments in this book however, I urge you to seriously consider some form of investment and periodically allocate some funds to it. The general misconception is that you need to have a lot of money to invest but I challenge that idea by stating – if you want to potentially have more money, you need to consider investing and letting your money work for you, even while you sleep. Money put in investments are not FDIC insured and therefore there is no guarantee of not losing your money if you make the wrong decision. This statement or a variation of it will feature in almost every text referring to investments. You should not be scared of the warning. Research your investments properly and diversify your investment (invest in different companies, sectors, markets, etc.). Even if you do not have a lot of money, you can still be diversified in certain Exchange Traded Funds (ETFs) and/or mutual funds. These are investment vehicles that generally include multiple companies under one umbrella of the ETF or mutual fund you buy.

Budgeting leads to better savings and investments potentially lead to better growth. Consider a scenario where you tweaked your budget and realized a $200 savings a month. What if you invested that $200 a month for 17 years at 5% average annualized returns? At the end of 17 years, you will have accumulated over $64,000 with over $23,000 of this amount resulting from interest growth. Even after an estimated 15% capital gains tax, you still end up with about $20,000 in accrued interest. If you had a baby when you started contributing to your investments, that money could go toward college expenses 17+ years later.

It takes time for money to grow. You will not get rich overnight but you should stay the course and build wealth over the long term.

There is a well known rule called the rule of 72; If you divide 72 by an expected annual rate of return, you will get a rough estimate of how long it takes to double your initial investment.

At 5% rate of return (ROR) it would take approximately 72 / 5 = 14years to double an initial investment. At 6% ROR, it will take approximately 72 / 6 = 12 years.

Tips:

A few tips are outlined below to help you achieve cost savings and put more into savings and investments

Groceries:

1. Make a list and stick to it (stick to your budget too).
2. Buy fruits and vegetables in season, they are usually cheaper. If you find a great fruit sale, buy in bulk, clean and freeze to use later.
3. Look for the price per unit (price per item, per ounce, per pound). If two brands of canned tomatoes for example, have different prices, the can with the lowest price per ounce (oz) will be cheaper per unit. Even if the other can has a lower overall price tag.
4. Items at the bottom of the shelves are usually cheaper than those at eye level.
5. Check the store ad for coupons and sales.
6. Ask for a rain check if an item on sale is not available. You can use it to buy the item at the same price later on.
7. Buy meats and seafood on sale and freeze them.
8. Consider buying the store brand. These are generally cheaper.

Around the house:

1. Decrease water heater temperature, raise thermostat temperature (summer), lower thermostat temperature (winter), increase refrigerator/freezer temperature (coldest might not be necessary), use energy efficient bulbs. All these will yield both energy and cost savings.
2. Learn to be handy and take care of minor repairs at home. There are instructional videos online for almost everything.
3. Self service – cut your own lawn, hair, etc. and pay yourself for it.
4. Shop for the best electricity/internet/cable service, avoid blindly renewing any contracts.
5. Get rid of cable. You will not miss it (that much).

4   BUYING A HOUSE

A new chapter in your life is about to begin. You are considering buying a house. Like many of us, you may not have a war chest full of cash to outright pay for the house and be done with it, so you have come to the right place. What we aim to accomplish here is to talk about some options available to help you finance the purchase of your home, then we will look at some other factors to consider prior to purchasing your home to ensure you are making a sound financial decision. These options or mortgages can be subdivided into two major categories: fixed and variable interest rate mortgages.

Any loan taken has an interest rate associated with repayment and mortgages are no different. In the case of a fixed interest rate mortgage, the interest rate stays the same for the life of your mortgage therefore; your payments will be the same for the term of your mortgage. "Term" as used here is the length of time you and the lender agreed you will make a series of payments until the balance you owe is zero. Typical terms for fixed interest rate mortgages are 15 or 30 years.

Adjustable rate mortgages (ARM) as the name implies, have interest rates that are not fixed (they vary) through the term of the loan. Most of the adjustable rate mortgages available today are actually more of a combination of the fixed and variable rate types. Typical terms for this type of mortgage are 15 or 30 years. Examples of adjustable rate mortgages are 5/1 ARM and 3/1 ARM. In these cases, the interest rate is fixed for a specified period of time – 5 years for a 5/1 ARM and 3 years for a 3/1 ARM, after which, the interest rate will change at most once a year – represented by the "1" in 5/1 and 3/1 ARM respectively.

4.1 COMMON TYPES OF MORTGAGES

There are other types of loans such as conventional, FHA (Federal Housing Administration), VA (Veterans Affairs), Jumbo loans. As mentioned above, all these loan types can have adjustable or fixed interest rates.

4.1.1 CONVENTIONAL MORTGAGE

Conventional mortgages are loans that meet guidelines set by Fannie Mae and Freddie Mac, both government sponsored enterprises. These loans are not guaranteed by the federal government. Conventional mortgages should generally be used by borrowers with very good credit scores and who also have the required minimum down payment. Minimum required down payment for most loans is 20%. Conventional loans also have the option of down payments as low as 5%, however, any conventional mortgage with less than a 20% down payment will require the borrower to pay a Private Mortgage Insurance (PMI) premium.

PMI is insurance that is paid for by you the borrower, to ensure that the bank or lender does not lose money in case you default on the loan. Note that the PMI, even though paid by you, is not for your protection. The lender assumes that giving you a mortgage when you have less than the 20% of the cost of the house to use as a down payment is an additional risk and generally require you to carry this insurance for their protection. Think as far back as you can remember…have you ever bought or paid for an insurance premium when the insurance offered you no protection whatsoever? Probably not, but in the world of mortgages, this is the reality.

The question "How do I get rid of this PMI given it is insurance that does not help or protect me?" arises. Let us introduce the concept of loan-to-value (LTV). Imagine you took out a conventional mortgage and made a 10% down payment, you are taking a 90% (100% - 10% down payment) loan on the value of the house. Therefore your LTV is 90%. To avoid PMI, you need at least an LTV of 80%, thus a 20% down payment required.

If you are currently paying PMI on a conventional mortgage, you can request your lender to remove PMI when you reach 80% LTV. This will likely have to be a written request so check with your lender and ask if additional information is required for you to submit. Once you reach an LTV of 78%, your lender is required to drop PMI even without a formal/informal request from you.

Another method to calculate LTV is to divide the value of the house by the loan balance.

For example, you bought your current house for $250,000, you put down 10% ($25,000) and took out a conventional mortgage which to date you have paid $20,000 toward the principal. You house currently appraises for $270,000.

$$LTV = \frac{loan\ balance}{home\ value}$$

Original Loan amount = Purchase price – down payment

$$= \$250,000 - \$25,000$$

$$= \$225,000$$

Current Loan balance = Original loan amount – principal payment to date

$$= \$225,000 - \$20,000$$

$$= \$205,000$$

$$\text{LTV} = \frac{\$205,000}{\$270,000} = 0.76 \text{ or } 76\%$$

You would think that with time and your house appreciating in value, you would reach the 80% LTV faster. While this is true, lenders generally will consider the loan balance relative to the original purchase price of the house for existing conventional loans per the mortgage documentation which will yield a lower LTV. Considering the LTV of 76% calculated above, if the original purchase price is used, the LTV would be 82% ($205,000/$250,000) and you will be required to continue paying PMI. In this case, refinancing your mortgage may be an option to get rid of PMI. There are other factors to consider before refinancing such as interest rates, additional closing costs, refinance term, which are crucial to evaluate to ensure you are making the right financial decision. We will examine these later on.

4.1.2 FHA MORTGAGES

FHA mortgages are loans for which there is a guaranty by the federal government. FHA mortgages are typically taken by home buyers who do not have a very good credit score and have less than the required 20% down payment. The minimum credit score required is about 580. Down payments for FHA loans are a minimum 3.5% of the purchase price of the house. The lower credit score required to qualify for FHA loans is interpreted by lenders as the loans being riskier. Excellent credit scores (720 and up) indicate to lenders that you manage debt very well and are likely to pay them back. As credit scores decrease, the increase in perceived risk by lenders, leads interest rates for borrowers with lower credit scores to be higher. However, with FHA loans, your interest rate could be lower than with conventional loans. This already sounds great right? Maybe so, but we do not yet have the whole picture on FHA mortgages. Remember PMI? FHA loans also have something similar for buyers with less than 20% down payment called Mortgage Insurance Premium (MIP). MIP similar to PMI above for conventional loans is there to protect the lender from any default in payments by the borrower. To clarify, lender as used above includes the original entity or financial institution that made the loan to the borrower, as well as any investor(s) who subsequently bought the mortgage (debt).

An upfront MIP payment (a percentage of the amount borrowed), is required to be paid as well as an annual MIP. Currently, the upfront rate is 1.75% of the borrowed amount and about an average of 0.85% of the loan balance annually. Now you see that further research is required in order to make the right decision on if to select an FHA mortgage. The upfront fee can either be paid or financed with the loan. Remember, just because something can be done does not mean you should do it! If you chose to finance the upfront fee with your mortgage, you would be paying an overall higher amount throughout the term of the loan due to the loan interest rate which will always be greater than 0%.

It is worth also clarifying that the Federal Housing Administration (FHA) itself does not give loans, they only guaranty them. Prospective borrowers will have to go to a private lender offering FHA loan products. Stay with me, we will get through these housekeeping items and get into some examples with numbers. However, it is imperative that we all understand what each mortgage type offers.

4.1.3   VETERANS AFFAIRS (VA) MORTGAGES

The VA loans, similar to the FHA loans are provided by private lenders and not the VA itself. However, the VA does provide a guaranty for these loans. Veterans, active duty service members and certain surviving spouses can qualify for a VA loan.

For eligibility and additional information, refer to the VA website at http://www.benefits.va.gov/homeloans/. Some of the benefits of a VA mortgage are: no down payment required; no PMI required; potentially low interest rates.

4.2   DEBT TO INCOME RATIO (DTI)

Imagine a situation (maybe you can relate to this) where a family member who picks up odd gigs here and there constantly borrows money from relatives and seldom repays them. This family member approaches you and asks for a loan. Do you give them the loan? I know there is no unanimous "NO" answer to this question because this person is still family but even if you give that loan, you likely have accepted that you will never get that money back!

When lenders give out loans, they want to ensure that you are not like the family member mentioned above. Unlike family, lenders have no emotional ties and will not provide you with a loan if they think you are unlikely to pay them back. The more debts you have, the less likely it is you can repay an additional loan.

Debt to income ratio is calculated by adding all your monthly debt payments and dividing that by your gross monthly income. You can research more on DTIs, Front-End and Back-End ratios but we will consider only the definition above, which aligns with the back-end DTI. Front-end DTIs consider only mortgage payment divided by gross monthly income and in my opinion does not give a good overall picture.

Lenders generally limit the DTI to about 43%. Above this point, lenders consider the borrower to be more likely to run into difficulties paying the mortgage and will likely not qualify for a loan. Why is this important to know? It is imperative that you are well prepared and informed before committing to any debt. Just because lenders limit the DTI to 43% does not imply in your analysis to determine how much house you can afford you should go all the way to 43%. Aim to keep your DTI as low as possible so you still have funds to save and invest in your future.

Example: Jane has a monthly gross income of $6,500 and a monthly debt payment (mortgage, credit cards, car payments, student loan payments, etc.) of $2,600. Jane's DTI is 40% ($2,600/$6,500).

If you are doing your own DTI analysis, take into consideration the fact that the DTI formula uses gross income, this implies it does not take into consideration that you will have payroll tax deductions (federal tax, state tax, social security tax, Medicare tax), and additional deductions such as pretax premiums for medical, dental and vision insurance and contributions to retirement accounts (e.g. 401K). If you consider these deductions from your gross pay and use a modified DTI ratio considering your actual take home pay, this would give you a more realistic picture of your financial situation before taking on a mortgage or any additional debt.

Assume Jane is a Texas resident, single, contributes 10% to her 401K and has a monthly total insurance payment of $150 deducted from her paycheck. An estimate of her deductions is as follows:

Gross monthly pay: $6,500

Taxes (Federal, Medicare, Social security): $1,461.78

401K: $650

Insurance: $150

Monthly take home (net) pay: $4,238.22 ($6,500 - $1,461.78 - $650 - $150)

Modified DTI based on net monthly income is 61% ($2,600/ $4,238.78).

For your analysis, I recommend using the modified DTI method because it gives you the most accurate picture. In Jane's case, the modified DTI is 61%, implying that after paying off all her monthly debts, Jane will be left with 39% (100% - 61%) of her take home pay or $1,652.90.

4.3   OTHER ITEMS TO CONSIDER BEFORE TAKING A MORTGAGE

One thing you should always remember is to look at your finances as a whole prior to any changes; long or short term. On that note, there are several things you should also consider before taking a mortgage.

4.3.1   INTEREST RATE

Shopping for the best interest rate on your mortgage is definitely a must as this will either cost or save you a lot. The seller may have a preferred lender but you should shop around to see if you can find a better interest rate that would offset any upfront benefits that the preferred lender is offering such as paying part or all of your closing costs. To quantify the impact of interest rate, consider a 30 year $200,000 mortgage at 4% versus 3.75%. The loan at 3.75% over 30 years will cost about $10,000 less in interest payments. If you could secure a loan at 3.125% relative to the 4%, the interest cost savings are about $35,000!

4.3.2   CURRENT/FUTURE INCOME

It goes without saying that you should be able to afford your mortgage before signing any documents to buy a home. If you are married, I recommend you use the income of the lower earning spouse and ensure it covers all your monthly debt obligations with some room for saving. This will give your family better odds of weathering any financial storm should the higher income earner lose their job. Plus, this will also give you some flexibility to save and invest in your future.

4.3.3   FUTURE DEBT

You should also allow some room to repay any future debts such as student loans, car note, child care expenses, etc. While these may not be in the picture when you buy your house, remember that a mortgage is a very long term commitment, 15 to 30 years and other financial obligations are likely to overlap this time period.

If you have ever told yourself "I'll cross that bridge when I get there", you should plan better as to what you will do if and when that moment in life comes. Leaving it up to fate is illogical and will likely lead to more stress later on.

MISCELLANEOUS ITEMS

Keep some room in your budget for other expenses such as:

- Vacations
- Home projects/ maintenance
- Increase in property taxes as home appreciates in value
- Increase in insurance premiums

4.4 MORTGAGE OPTIONS ANALYSIS (EXAMPLES)

Given all the information covered so far, we shall now look at a few examples to see how we can evaluate the different mortgage options. For this, we will take a snap shot of sample interest rates offered by a financial institution for the different types of loans discussed above:

MORTGAGE TYPE	INTEREST RATE*
30-year fixed rate	3.75%
30-year fixed rate – FHA	3.75%
15-year fixed rate	3.00%
7/1 ARM	3.25%

These are not the Annual Percentage Rate (APR). APR includes associated loan fees which vary per lender. Lender will use APR for these calculations.

4.4.1 EXAMPLE 1: CONVENTIONAL OR FHA LOAN SELECTION

Jane is about to purchase a home for $250,000 and she would rather have a lower monthly contractual payment so she wants a 30 year mortgage. Her down payment is 7% or $17,500 ($250,000 x 0.07). Should she choose a conventional or an FHA loan? Assume she has good enough credit to qualify for both types of loans.

If you looked at the interest rates listed in the table, realized they were the same and said "it doesn't matter what Jane selects!" I would recommend you remember PMI and MIP given that Jane's down payment is less than 20%. Her LTV is 93%, so for either loan, she will be paying mortgage insurance.

House Price: $250,000

Down payment: $17,500

Loan Amount: $232,500

Interest rate: 3.75%

OPTION A: Jane selects a conventional 30-year fixed interest rate mortgage

PMI estimate: 0.75% (There are several online calculators to help estimate PMI)

Remember: for conventional loans, PMI can be removed at LTV of 80%. In this example, that will happen 3 months shy of completing her 7th year of payment. Use an online amortization calculator to see the monthly breakdown. A summary of her 30 year annual amortization is given below. Note that we simplified PMI calculations by keeping monthly PMI constant through year 7. Actual PMI calculations will consider the average annual balance on the loan which will decrease this amount slightly. However, since this is just an estimate anyway, we will proceed with a constant PMI.

Year	Payments	Principal Paid	Interest Paid	PMI	Principal Balance (Year End)
					$232,500.00
1	$14,664.63	$4,275.11	$8,645.77	$1,743.75	$228,224.89
2	$14,664.63	$4,438.21	$8,482.67	$1,743.75	$223,786.68
3	$14,664.63	$4,607.55	$8,313.33	$1,743.75	$219,179.13
4	$14,664.63	$4,783.34	$8,137.54	$1,743.75	$214,395.79

Year	Payments	Principal Paid	Interest Paid	PMI	Principal Balance (Year End)
5	$14,664.63	$4,965.80	$7,955.08	$1,743.75	$209,429.99
6	$14,664.63	$5,155.25	$7,765.63	$1,743.75	$204,274.74
7	$14,228.69	$5,351.95	$7,568.93	$1,307.81	$198,922.79
8	$12,920.88	$5,556.15	$7,364.73	-	$193,366.64
9	$12,920.88	$5,768.10	$7,152.78	-	$187,598.54
10	$12,920.88	$5,988.15	$6,932.73	-	$181,610.39
11	$12,920.88	$6,216.63	$6,704.25	-	$175,393.76
12	$12,920.88	$6,453.79	$6,467.09	-	$168,939.97
13	$12,920.88	$6,700.00	$6,220.88	-	$162,239.97
14	$12,920.88	$6,955.64	$5,965.24	-	$155,284.33
15	$12,920.88	$7,220.99	$5,699.89	-	$148,063.34
16	$12,920.88	$7,496.48	$5,424.40	-	$140,566.86
17	$12,920.88	$7,782.46	$5,138.42	-	$132,784.40
18	$12,920.88	$8,079.39	$4,841.49	-	$124,705.01
19	$12,920.88	$8,387.64	$4,533.24	-	$116,317.37
20	$12,920.88	$8,707.64	$4,213.24	-	$107,609.73
21	$12,920.88	$9,039.82	$3,881.06	-	$98,569.91
22	$12,920.88	$9,384.72	$3,536.16	-	$89,185.19
23	$12,920.88	$9,742.76	$3,178.12	-	$79,442.43
24	$12,920.88	$10,114.46	$2,806.42	-	$69,327.97
25	$12,920.88	$10,500.32	$2,420.56	-	$58,827.65
26	$12,920.88	$10,900.92	$2,019.96	-	$47,926.73
27	$12,920.88	$11,316.84	$1,604.04	-	$36,609.89
28	$12,920.88	$11,748.56	$1,172.32	-	$24,861.33
29	$12,920.88	$12,196.80	$724.08	-	$12,664.53
30	$12,923.29	$12,664.53	$258.76		$0.00

A chart of the principal balance and interest payment over the 30 year mortgage term is presented next.

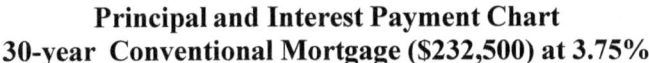

Principal and Interest Payment Chart
30-year Conventional Mortgage ($232,500) at 3.75%

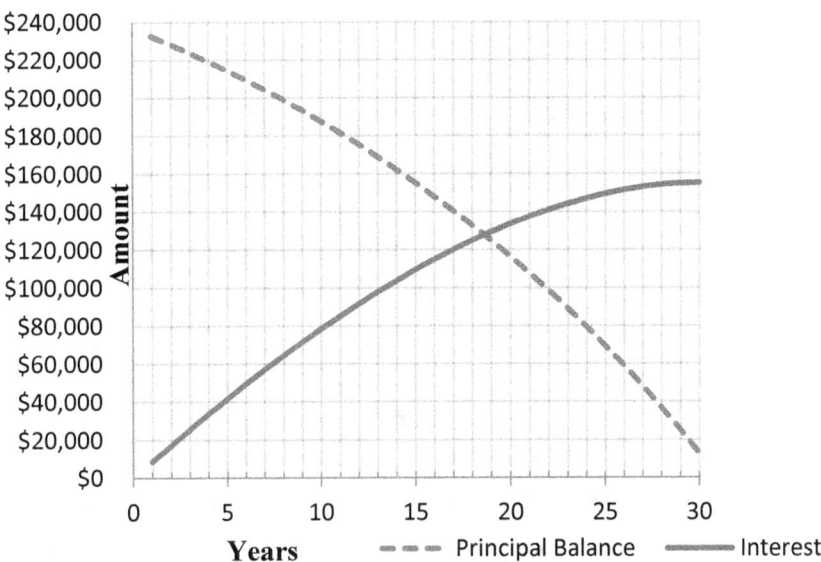

SUMMARY

Description	Amount	Comment
Monthly Payment	$1,076.74	Principal and interest only
Monthly PMI	$145.31	-
Total PMI	$11,770.31	-
Total Interest Paid	$155,128.81	-
Total amount Paid	$387,628.81	-

Notice that the interest paid back over 30 years is about 67% of the amount borrowed. There are additional things Jane could do to decrease the overall interest paid such as making additional monthly payment to her principal balance, or annual payments to principal. Tax refunds are a good source of money for additional payments to principal. If you take a look at the amortization table, you will notice that the bulk of interest payments are at the beginning of the loan. Therefore to actually decrease the amount of interest paid, additional payments should be made as early as possible.

A short analysis before we move along to option B.

If Jane decided to consistently:

    i)   Add $50 a month toward her principal, she would save almost $14,000 in interest and pay off the loan about 2 years earlier

    ii)   Add $100 a month toward her principal, she would save over $25,000 in interest and pay off the loan about 4 years earlier

    iii)   Add $300 a month toward her principal, she would save almost $57,000 in interest and pay off the loan about 10 years earlier

We will revisit the discussion on additional payments to principal after discussing the 15 year mortgage option.

There is one more chart we should look at before proceeding to option B. This shows how the total principal and interest payments fluctuate over the term of the loan.

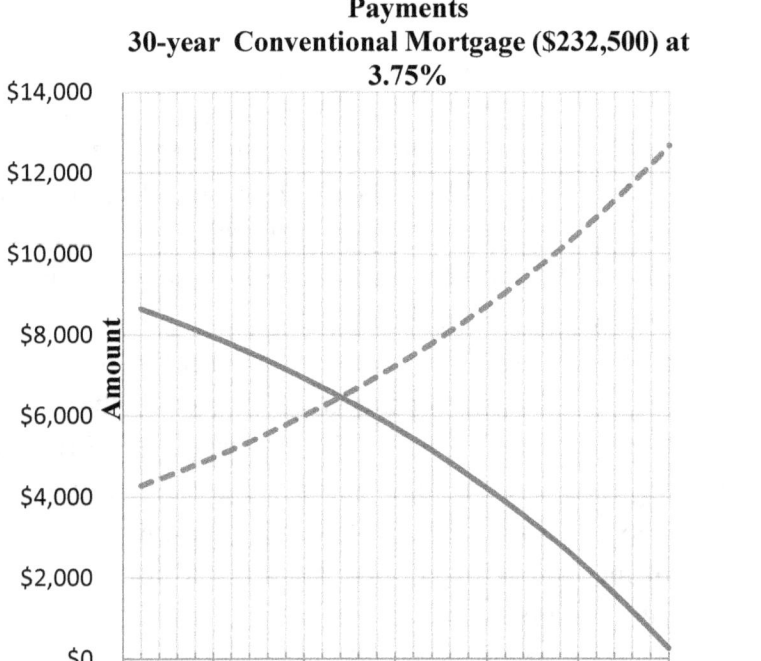

Changes in Annual Principal and Interest Payments
30-year Conventional Mortgage ($232,500) at 3.75%

The point of intersection in the chart indicates when Jane's payments to principal will equal her interest payments. A larger portion of monthly payments go towards interest until the 12th year into the 30 year mortgage. Interest is calculated based on the principal balance. In order to decrease the total interest paid over the life of the loan, the point of intersection needs to be moved toward the left as much as possible or be eliminated altogether. This can be done by making additional payments to principal much earlier in the life of the loan.

OPTION B: Jane selects an FHA 30-year fixed interest rate mortgage

The interest rates for options A and B above are the same; however, MIP rules are different for FHA mortgages. An upfront MIP payment of 1.75% of the borrowed amount is required ($232,500 x 0.0175 = $4,068.75). Since Jane's LTV is 93%, per the FHA guidelines the monthly PMI rate is 0.8%. (Always check FHA guidelines as these may change). Since Jane has $17,500 available to make a down payment, for this calculation we will combine her upfront MIP with the $232,500 (loan amount) and finance the total $236,568.75. New FHA loans with MIP require the borrower to keep the insurance for the life of the mortgage. Our PMI calculation below considers the average annual principal balance approach because the principal balance eventually gets low enough through the life of the loan. The 0.8% of the principal balance will yield a significantly different result at the start of the loan compared to the middle or final years.

House Price: $250,000

Down payment: $17,500

Upfront MIP: $4,068.75 (1.75% of $232,500)

Loan Amount: $232,500 + $4,068.75 = $236,568.75

Interest rate: 3.75%

MIP annual rate: 0.8%

Year	Payments	Principal Paid	Interest Paid	MIP	Principal Balance (Year End)
					$236,569.00
1	$14,991.51	$4,350.00	$8,797.08	$1,844.43	$232,219.00
2	$14,956.72	$4,515.96	$8,631.12	$1,809.64	$227,703.04
3	$14,920.59	$4,688.25	$8,458.83	$1,773.51	$223,014.79
4	$14,883.09	$4,867.11	$8,279.97	$1,736.01	$218,147.68
5	$14,844.16	$5,052.82	$8,094.26	$1,697.08	$213,094.86
6	$14,803.74	$5,245.58	$7,901.50	$1,656.66	$207,849.28
7	$14,761.78	$5,445.69	$7,701.39	$1,614.70	$202,403.59
8	$14,718.22	$5,653.46	$7,493.62	$1,571.14	$196,750.13
9	$14,673.00	$5,869.15	$7,277.93	$1,525.92	$190,880.98
10	$14,626.06	$6,093.05	$7,054.03	$1,478.98	$184,787.93
11	$14,577.32	$6,325.51	$6,821.57	$1,430.24	$178,462.42
12	$14,526.72	$6,566.83	$6,580.25	$1,379.64	$171,895.59
13	$14,474.19	$6,817.38	$6,329.70	$1,327.11	$165,078.21
14	$14,419.66	$7,077.46	$6,069.62	$1,272.58	$158,000.75
15	$14,363.05	$7,347.50	$5,799.58	$1,215.97	$150,653.25
16	$14,304.28	$7,627.79	$5,519.29	$1,157.20	$143,025.46
17	$14,243.26	$7,918.81	$5,228.27	$1,096.18	$135,106.65
18	$14,179.92	$8,220.92	$4,926.16	$1,032.84	$126,885.73
19	$14,114.16	$8,534.56	$4,612.52	$967.08	$118,351.17
20	$14,045.90	$8,860.17	$4,286.91	$898.82	$109,491.00
21	$13,975.03	$9,198.21	$3,948.87	$827.95	$100,292.79
22	$13,901.45	$9,549.12	$3,597.96	$754.37	$90,743.67
23	$13,825.07	$9,913.42	$3,233.66	$677.99	$80,830.25
24	$13,745.77	$10,291.63	$2,855.45	$598.69	$70,538.62
25	$13,663.45	$10,684.28	$2,462.80	$516.37	$59,854.34
26	$13,577.99	$11,091.90	$2,055.18	$430.91	$48,762.44
27	$13,489.26	$11,515.06	$1,632.02	$342.18	$37,247.38
28	$13,397.16	$11,954.38	$1,192.70	$250.08	$25,293.00
29	$13,301.53	$12,410.46	$736.62	$154.45	$12,882.54
30	$13,202.26	$12,882.54	$263.13	$55.18	$0.00

The chart next, depicts how the total balance of the principal, interest and MIP change over the mortgage term.

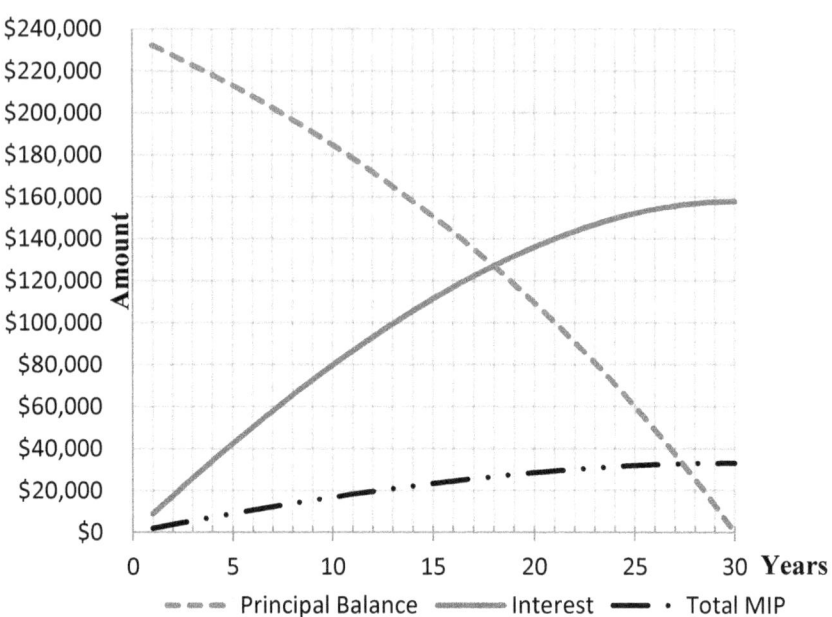

Principal, Interest & MIP Payment Chart
30-year FHA Mortgage ($232,500) at 3.75%

SUMMARY

Description (FHA)	Amount	Comment
Monthly Payment	$1,095.59	Principal and interest only
Monthly MIP	Varies	Divide values in table above by 12
Total MIP Paid	$33,093.92	-
Total Interest Paid	$157,841.99	-
Total amount Paid	$427,506.32	-

For a quick comparison, the summary table from the conventional loan option is shown next.

Description	Amount	Comment
Monthly Payment	$1,076.74	Principal and interest only
Monthly PMI	$145.31	-
Total PMI	$11,770.31	-
Total Interest Paid	$155,128.81	-
Total amount Paid	$387,628.81	-

Since the upfront FHA MIP was financed with the loan amount, the total interest paid is almost $3,000 more than the conventional loan option. However, the MIP on the FHA loan stays for the entire loan term. The FHA loan MIP is more than $21,000 higher than the PMI for the conventional loan. The FHA loan will also cost you about $40,000 more over a 30-year term.

It is clear from this analysis that the conventional loan is definitely the way to go.

In general, you should always choose a conventional loan if you qualify for it. Even if the interest rate is the same as an FHA loan, the MIP will end up costing you more money. The upfront MIP on the FHA loan is also an additional cost.

4.4.2   EXAMPLE 2: LENGTH OF MORTGAGE TERM

We have answered the question on what mortgage should be selected between the FHA and conventional mortgage. What if Jane was considering a 15 year mortgage? How does this compare to taking a 30 year conventional mortgage?

The table below gives the annual amortization for a 15 year mortgage. We will use the same down payment and PMI information as above. Interest rates used is 3% as reported in the interest rate table at the beginning of this section.

15 year conventional mortgage annual amortization schedule

Year	Payments	Principal Paid	Interest Paid	PMI	Principal Balance (Year End)
					$232,500.00
1	$21,010.95	$12,462.63	$6,804.57	$1,743.75	$220,037.37
2	$21,010.95	$12,841.70	$6,425.50	$1,743.75	$207,195.67
3	$19,703.14	$13,232.30	$6,034.90	$435.94	$193,963.37
4	$19,267.20	$13,634.76	$5,632.44	-	$180,328.61
5	$19,267.20	$14,049.48	$5,217.72	-	$166,279.13
6	$19,267.20	$14,476.81	$4,790.39	-	$151,802.32
7	$19,267.20	$14,917.12	$4,350.08	-	$136,885.20
8	$19,267.20	$15,370.87	$3,896.33	-	$121,514.33
9	$19,267.20	$15,838.36	$3,428.84	-	$105,675.97
10	$19,267.20	$16,320.11	$2,947.09	-	$89,355.86
11	$19,267.20	$16,816.49	$2,450.71	-	$72,539.37
12	$19,267.20	$17,327.98	$1,939.22	-	$55,211.39
13	$19,267.20	$17,855.04	$1,412.16	-	$37,356.35
14	$19,267.20	$18,398.12	$869.08	-	$18,958.23
15	$19,267.73	$18,958.23	$309.50	-	$0.00

SUMMARY

	15 yr mortgage	30 yr mortgage	
Description	Amount	Amount	Comment
Monthly Payment	$1,605.60	$1,076.74	Principal and interest only
Monthly PMI	$145.31	$145.31	-
Total PMI Paid	$3,923.44	$11,770.31	-
Total Interest Paid	$56,508.53	$155,128.81	-
Total amount Paid	$292,931.97	$387,628.81	-

For easy comparison, the values for both the 15 and 30-year mortgages are presented in the table above.

The total interest paid with a 15 year mortgage is about $100,000 less than with a 30 year mortgage. This is due to the lower interest rate associated with the 15 year mortgage and also because the 15 year mortgage requires larger monthly payments made to the principal.

Based on the summary table, you should definitely select a 15 year mortgage over a 30 year mortgage if you can afford it.

If 15-year mortgages are less costly, why are 30 year mortgages more popular than 15 year mortgages? The answer to this lies in the bigger picture. First of all the monthly payments shown in the table above do not reflect the true monthly payments if you have an escrow account. An escrow account is an account created by your lender to collect your homeowner's insurance premiums and taxes monthly, and at the end of the year your lender makes these payments on your behalf. If an escrow account is set up by your lender, your monthly mortgage payment will be increased by an amount equal to the sum of your homeowner's insurance plus anticipated property taxes divided by 12 (months).

In the example above, the minimum monthly contractual obligation for a 30 year mortgage is about $528 less than with a 15 year mortgage. This lower contractual obligation allows borrowers additional room in their budgets to meet short and long term obligations and plan for things like retirement, additional savings, unemployment, kids, new vehicle, etc. A mortgage is a long term financial commitment and many changes to your financial situation will occur in 15 and/or 30 years. You should consider this carefully before selecting your mortgage term.

For first time homebuyers, I recommend you select a 30 year mortgage and take advantage of the lower minimum contractual payment. If you can afford the payment amount for a 15 year mortgage, you can pay the additional $528 monthly toward the loan principal of a 30 year mortgage in the previous example. Your interest payments will still be higher than with a 15 year mortgage due to the higher interest rate, but if you unfailingly pay this amount throughout the life of the loan, instead of the $155,128.81 total interest paid for a 30 year loan, your interest payment would be cut down to $77,566, about 50% less. Your loan will also be paid off entirely in a little over 16 years.

This option gives you flexibility in case of unfortunate or unpredictable life events such as a layoff or sickness, to be able to more comfortably meet a lower 30 year monthly minimum contractual obligation that is $528 less than with a corresponding 15 year loan. Yes you still end up paying more interest than with a 15 year mortgage but it seems a better route than risk losing your home should additional expenses such as the birth of a child, new car requirement or ailing spouse cause you to be financially strained and unable to make higher mortgage payments, including any escrow payments.

4.4.3 EXAMPLE 3: ARM VS CONVENTIONAL MORTGAGE (SHORT TERM)

Christel has found a home in a great neighborhood and anticipates staying there for maybe five to six years, sell the home and cash out the equity built within that time frame. The cost of the home is $300,000 and she has $60,000 as her 20% down payment. Will a 30 year adjustable rate mortgage (ARM) be a preferred option in this case or should she stick with a 30-year fixed interest loan?

The loan interest rates as same as listed above:

- 3.75% for a 30-year fixed interest rate conventional loan and
- 3.25% for a 7/1 ARM (30-year conventional) with a maximum interest rate increase of +/- 5%.

We know Christel plans to stay in the home for a maximum of 6 years. Given that the interest rate is lower for the 7/1 ARM, this would definitely be the better option to consider.

Remember: In the case of the 7/1 ARM, the 3.25% interest is fixed for the first seven years and the interest rate after that will change at most once a year, with a maximum change of 5% in this example.

Both mortgages are of the conventional type with a 20% down payment and therefore require no PMI. The selection of the ARM will lead to lower payments in interest for the first seven years.

To quantify the difference in interest payments, we shall make some assumptions: First, closing costs are same for both ARM and fixed interest mortgages and second, Christel successfully sells her home after 6 years of ownership.

The loan amount is $240,000 ($300,000 - $60,000)

	30 yr ARM	30 yr Fixed
Description	**Amount**	**Amount**
Total Interest (first six years)	$43,888	$50,890

Christel will pay about $7,000 less in interest with the 7/1 ARM compared to the 30 year fixed. Given her constraint of selling the house in maximum 6 years, the ARM is a better option.

CAUTION:

The ARM works in this scenario because we assumed that the house was sold before the interest rate starts to adjust. The truth is that reality does not always walk along the same path as our plans. Home values do decrease sometimes as in the case of the great economic recession in the United States in 2008. Many home owners found themselves in upside down mortgages, meaning the value of the house fell so much that the mortgage balance was higher than the value of the house. Any home owner in this situation who tries to sell their house will end up still owing their lender since the sale price of the house will not cover the mortgage balance. This is an example of a situation beyond your control that will likely affect the timeline you set to sell your home sometime in the future.

What if there are no parties interested in buying your house when you are ready to sell? Maybe because you were unaware that a rail track would later on be built close to your house. Now there is the concern of the train horn throughout the day and in the calm of the night when you attempt to sleep. You might then be forced to keep the ARM mortgage past the fixed interest rate period, likely making it a less attractive option. The ARM interest may also drop below the initial fixed rate but even if so, it likely would not be for long. My point here is that you do not have a crystal ball to predict the future. When considering an ARM, also consider the unknown beyond the fixed interest rate period and if you will be able to afford the mortgage should it spill into the adjustable rate term and reach the maximum interest rate according to the loan contract.

In the example with Christel above, at 3.25% her initial interest and principal payment is about $1,088. Since the rate adjustment is independent of her personal financial situation, if the interest rate were to increase to 5% in year 8, her monthly payment would be about $1,292, an increase of about 19%. At 7.5% interest on the loan balance after year 7, her payments would increase to about $1,613, a 48% increase compared to the initial fixed interest rate for the first seven years. This shows you a major downside of having an ARM and how your mortgage payments may spiral out of control and become too expensive for you to afford.

People have lost their homes before because of the faulty assumption that their interest rate will not increase to the maximum stated in the mortgage contract. Remember that your lender is interested in making as much money as possible on loans given out. If the underlying index your ARM is based on increases, your lender will likely not shield you from this increase when it is time for the annual rate adjustment. Evaluate the worst case scenario of any options you are considering and plan to weather these scenarios should you have to live through them. Your aim is always to minimize expenditure – keep that in mind.

4.5 REFINANCE

There are several reasons why someone might consider refinancing a mortgage. Some of them are:

- Decreasing mortgage interest rate
- Changing mortgage term
- Removing mortgage insurance premium
- Cashing out equity in your home

You should always do an evaluation of the overall cost of refinancing to determine if you should proceed. Example short term costs (if paid upfront) are closing costs and associated appraisal fees. Long term costs would be the additional interests if any that would be incurred if you refinance.

4.5.1   DECREASING MORTGAGE INTEREST RATE

One of the main reasons to refinance a mortgage is to secure a lower interest rate on the loan balance. A lower interest rate applied to a loan term equal to or less than the leftover term of an existing loan to be refinanced will lead to lower monthly payments. There is a diminishing return if you chose to refinance at a lower interest rate for a longer term. Even though your monthly payments will decrease, because of the increase in the loan term, your overall interest payment might be greater than with the original loan. A decrease in the market interest rates or improvement in personal credit score may present a good opportunity to consider refinancing.

4.5.2   CHANGE MORTGAGE TERM

People also refinance their mortgages in order to change the payment term. In addition to securing a lower interest rate, home owners can also opt to decrease the term of their mortgage to be lower than the remaining time on the original loan. This will lead to higher monthly payments as the principal will be paid off faster and the overall interest paid will be lower. Increasing the loan term and monthly payment through refinancing can be done but should be avoided because this option usually leads to paying more interest.

4.5.3   REMOVING MORTGAGE INSURANCE PREMIUMS

Mortgage insurance premiums are required to be kept until you have at least 20% equity in the home (owe 80% or less) for conventional loans and are required for the entire term on FHA loans. If your home value has appreciated significantly enough that your LTV with the new appraised value is less than 80% you may be able to take advantage of this to refinance. An official appraisal will be required. Contact your lender or potential lender(s) to find out if this is a viable option for you.

4.5.4   CASHING OUT EQUITY IN YOUR HOME

The value of your home, less any mortgage balance is the equity in your home. Your home equity increases as you pay down your principal balance and/or as your home value appreciates. For various reasons such as paying for college or home improvement projects, homeowners choose to cash out equity from their home. They refinance their house for an amount greater than the mortgage balance. The amount of money refinanced minus the previous mortgage balance is the equity the homeowner is cashing out from the home. This type of refinance is called cash out refinance.

4.5.5   EXAMPLE: REFINANCE EVALUATION

Francis took a $200,000 30 year mortgage at 6% interest and bought a house. There is no PMI associated with the mortgage. At the end of 10 years, he is considering refinancing his mortgage. He qualifies for a 5% interest rate on a 15 year mortgage offered by a lender with an estimated upfront closing cost of $3,000. By how much does he decrease his interest payments and should he refinance?

We will start by looking at the amortization table for the original loan amount of $200,000 at 6%. The information we need from this table is:

1. How much interest has Francis paid after 10 years.
2. How much interest will he have paid over the entire 30-year mortgage term.
3. Loan principal balance at the start of year 11 (amount to be refinanced).

Subtracting interest paid to date at the end of 10 years from total interest to be paid in 30 years will give the balance in interest payments due for the remainder of the 30-year mortgage term. We will compare this amount to the calculated interest Francis will pay

43

by refinancing the balance at the start of year 11 of the 30 year amortization in a 15 year mortgage.

$200,000 at 6% Annual Amortization for 30 years

Year	Payments	Principal Paid	Interest Paid	Interest (Total)	Principal Balance (Year End)
					$200,000
1	$14,389	$2,456	$11,933	$11,933	$197,544
2	$14,389	$2,607	$11,782	$23,715	$194,937
3	$14,389	$2,768	$11,621	$35,336	$192,168
4	$14,389	$2,939	$11,450	$46,786	$189,229
5	$14,389	$3,120	$11,269	$58,055	$186,109
6	$14,389	$3,313	$11,076	$69,131	$182,796
7	$14,389	$3,517	$10,872	$80,003	$179,279
8	$14,389	$3,734	$10,655	$90,658	$175,545
9	$14,389	$3,964	$10,425	$101,083	$171,580
10	$14,389	$4,209	$10,180	*$111,264*	*$167,372*
11	$14,389	$4,468	$9,921	$121,184	$162,903
12	$14,389	$4,744	$9,645	$130,829	$158,159
13	$14,389	$5,037	$9,353	$140,182	$153,122
14	$14,389	$5,347	$9,042	$149,224	$147,775
15	$14,389	$5,677	$8,712	$157,936	$142,098
16	$14,389	$6,027	$8,362	$166,298	$136,071
17	$14,389	$6,399	$7,990	$174,288	$129,672
18	$14,389	$6,794	$7,595	$181,884	$122,878
19	$14,389	$7,213	$7,177	$189,060	$115,665
20	$14,389	$7,658	$6,732	$195,792	$108,008
21	$14,389	$8,130	$6,259	$202,051	$99,878
22	$14,389	$8,631	$5,758	$207,809	$91,246
23	$14,389	$9,164	$5,226	$213,034	$82,083
24	$14,389	$9,729	$4,660	$217,695	$72,354
25	$14,389	$10,329	$4,060	$221,755	$62,025
26	$14,389	$10,966	$3,423	$225,178	$51,059
27	$14,389	$11,642	$2,747	$227,925	$39,416

Year	Payments	Principal Paid	Interest Paid	Interest (Total)	Principal Balance (Year End)
28	$14,389	$12,360	$2,029	$229,954	$27,056
29	$14,389	$13,123	$1,266	$231,220	$13,933
30	$14,390	$13,933	$457	*$231,677*	$0

Monthly payment with 30 year mortgage = $14,390 / 12 = $1,199

Remaining interest after 10 years   = $231,677 - $111,264

$$= \$120,\ 413$$

The figures used for interest paid through the end of ten years, total interest paid with a 30 year mortgage and principal balance of the 30 year mortgage after 10 years of payments are emphasized in italics in the previous table.

$167,372 at 5% interest Annual Amortization for 15 years

Year	Payments	Principal Paid	Interest Paid	Interest (Total)	Principal Balance (End of Year)
					$167,372
1	$15,883	$7,689	$8,194	$8,194	$159,683
2	$15,883	$8,082	$7,801	$15,995	$151,601
3	$15,883	$8,496	$7,387	$23,382	$143,105
4	$15,883	$8,930	$6,952	$30,334	$134,175
5	$15,883	$9,387	$6,496	$36,830	$124,787
6	$15,883	$9,868	$6,015	$42,845	$114,920
7	$15,883	$10,372	$5,510	$48,355	$104,548
8	$15,883	$10,903	$4,980	$53,335	$93,644
9	$15,883	$11,461	$4,422	$57,757	$82,184
10	$15,883	$12,047	$3,836	$61,593	$70,136
11	$15,883	$12,664	$3,219	$64,812	$57,473

12	$15,883	$13,312	$2,571	$67,383	$44,161
13	$15,883	$13,993	$1,890	$69,274	$30,169
14	$15,883	$14,708	$1,174	$70,448	$15,460
15	$15,882	$15,460	$422	$70,870	$0

Total interest payment if refinanced at 5% for 15 years is $70,870, compared to the $120,413 if he continues with the 30 year mortgage. Refinancing will decrease the interest payments by almost $50,000.

In the case of the 15 year refinanced mortgage, monthly principal and interest payments will be about $1,324. The new payment will be $125 higher per month compared to the 30 year mortgage but the loan will be paid off five years earlier and cost $50,000 less than with a 30 year mortgage. The closing cost ($3,000) associated with refinancing his mortgage is relatively small, compared to the potential cost reduction.

To answer the original question on if he should refinance, Francis will have to assess his finances. If the additional $125 a month on principal and interest payments is within his budget then he should definitely refinance his 30 year mortgage to a 15 year mortgage.

In this example, we covered two reasons why people refinance: lower interest rate and change mortgage term. What if Francis wanted to keep his overall mortgage term the same in order to lower payments at 5% interest? What would be the result if he decided to refinance his loan for 30 years instead of 15 (increasing term) at a 5.5% rate? Do the analysis similar to what we just completed and see if you get similar results as below:

    a. Keeping overall term the same means he would refinance the loan for a 20 year term

Monthly principal and interest payment: $1,105 ($94 less than original payments)

Interest savings relative to 30 yr mortgage: just under $23,000

b. Refinancing to another 30 year mortgage at 5.5% interest

Monthly principal and interest payment: $950 ($249 less than original payments)

Interest savings relative to initial 30 yr mortgage: **NONE! IT will cost over $54,000 in additional interest payments to refinance to the longer term!**

In general, while refinancing to a longer term may decrease your monthly payments, it is not recommended because it will likely lead to paying more interest overall on the loan, even if the interest rate is lower.

5   DEBT MANAGEMENT

Now let's talk about the elephant in the room – debt. People get into debt for various reasons, some good, others, well... In this section we will discuss things to consider before taking on debt and what to do with the debt you already have.

I mentioned before that the reasons for taking on debt maybe good or not so great. Consider two scenarios; in the first scenario, Jane takes out a $15,000 student loan to supplement her educational expenses and estimates once she enters the workforce, she will be able to payoff that debt in 5 years, using no more than 10% of her monthly income. In the second scenario, John sells his perfectly functioning car with a $10,000 loan balance and buys a luxury vehicle, increasing his overall debt to $55,000. Who do you think made the smarter decision Jane or John? If you fancied yourself driving a luxury vehicle and thought John made the smarter decision regarding debt, I am sorry to inform you that you guessed incorrectly. Why?

An investment in education generally leads to better paying jobs. In addition, with no more than 10% of her income, Jane will pay off her loan in less than 5 years and be debt free with more earning potential given her higher educational level and increase in work experience. John on the other hand, is experiencing continuous loss as the vehicle purchased loses value through depreciation. By the time John pays off the balance of his car loan, the car would be worth significantly less than its original purchase price. Jane invested in herself by getting an education – good reason in this case, while John consistently lost value throughout the length of time he owns the car as it depreciates.

Also note that taking a large student loan which will require a lifetime of payments because your job prospects post graduation do not pay well enough to service your debt is not a good financial decision. This leads us to the first part of our discussion on debt.

5.1 BEFORE TAKING ON DEBT

You need to be truthful to yourself if you are disciplined and responsible enough to take on debt and unfailingly pay it back. There are different scenarios where we would normally consider going into debt and we will look at evaluating a few of them after some housekeeping items.

Ideally, you should avoid debt by all means because you will generally pay back more than you borrowed. I say generally because certain debts for those with excellent credit scores might be at 0%. For overall financial wellbeing, you should minimize how much you pay out and maximize returns from various investments. Given that the world is not ideal, we will examine a few scenarios where we consider taking on debt.

5.1.1 STUDENT LOANS:

Emotions should NEVER play a part in the decision making process on whether or not to take a student loan or any debt. Note that even if you file for bankruptcy, your student loans will not be discharged. You will still be responsible for making payments to this debt. I bring this up to make a point that student loans will follow you to the grave if you are not careful in making decisions.

5.1.1.1 *THINGS TO CONSIDER BEFORE TAKING ON STUDENT LOANS*

-   College(s) you plan to attend
-   In-state or out of state public university

- Total cost of attendance (tuition, boarding, books, etc.)
- How much savings you have set aside for educational expenses
- How much you will have to borrow to cover cost
- Availability of other colleges/universities that provide a more affordable good quality education
- Working while going to school to cover some or all expenses
- Potential income post graduation
- If you can comfortably afford to pay off student loan debt post graduation and invest in your (family) future
- Maximum acceptable length of time to pay off your loans
- Volatility of your future career
- An alternate field or career path you are equally passionate about
- Loan interest rate

5.1.1.2   COLLEGES TO ATTEND

This is usually the relatively easier decision to make, governed by factors such as proximity to home, degree program you want to pursue, scholarships offered by schools, reputation and cost, to name a few. I would recommend you select at least two to three potential colleges/universities. Something I have to say here is that Community Colleges offer a way to take care of your freshman and sophomore level courses for a fraction of the cost of traditional four year institutions. Do your homework in evaluating this great option. I personally took this route and when I graduated with my bachelor's degree, I had virtually no debt! Whatever little debt I had was paid off within the first three months of starting my career. There are many who baselessly undervalue an education from a Community College. Remember – Emotions should **NEVER** play a part in this decision making process.

So, as a summary, we will use the table below to track the progress of our analysis. Feel free to build a more complex or simpler table, depending on factors considered.

Institution (College/University)	Option A	Option B	Option C

5.1.1.3 *IN-STATE OR OUT OF STATE UNIVERSITY*

If you are a resident of any state, your tuition at a public university will generally be less expensive within the state than if you were to choose a university that is located outside your state of residency. This decision alone will significantly affect the potential student loan debt you are likely to have upon graduation. For example, tuition for a first time freshman at an actual public university in Texas for 2017 is estimated at $311 per semester credit hour for a Texas resident versus $819 for a non Texas resident. For a degree requiring completion of 120 credit hours, tuition only, sums up to $37,320 ($311 x 120) for a resident and $98,280 ($819 x 120) for non residents. That is a difference of about $61,000! In the case of graduate students, the cost varies with in-state tuition costing on the low end about half of the out of state cost.

Given the above example, if you are to attend a public college/university, I urge you to consider staying within your state to take advantage of this lower in-state tuition rates. Also carry out a similar evaluation for private versus public schools as private schools tend to be more expensive. The purpose of this analysis is not to say that no one should attend a private or out of state university, the choice is ultimately yours but this will give you a better picture of the financial commitments you will likely incur with each option.

5.1.1.4   TOTAL COST OF ATTENDANCE

It is a little bit harder to get the exact dollar amount but you can get a very good estimate of the cost of attendance for many academic institutions. An estimated cost of attendance is generally provided on the university website with a breakdown showing cost of tuition, fees, room and board, etc. You can substitute the university's room and boarding expenses depending on if you plan to live off campus, have a roommate, live with family or any other alternative that will result in a different and hopefully lower overall cost. Degree plans are generally available online with information on the number of semester credit hours required for a particular degree. Find yours and multiply this number by the cost per credit hour to get your total estimated tuition through graduation. You should note that this is only an estimate as universities may increase tuition at their discretion.

Next, estimate the number of semesters it would take you to graduate by dividing the total credits required for your degree by the number of credit hours you plan to complete per semester. This number can be used to estimate additional fees such as student activity fees, if calculated as flat rate per semester. Get familiar with university fee policy, some may charge by semester credit hour (SCH). Other costs to be considered are for example lab fees or supplies for art courses. We will continue building on our table noted previously. This time we assume some total costs of attendance. For option C, we will assume you live with family and deduct an arbitrary boarding cost.

Institution (College/University)	Option A	Option B	Option C
Total Cost	$85,000	$95,000	$55,000

5.1.1.5 *SAVINGS SET ASIDE FOR EDUCATIONAL EXPENSES*

How much have you or your family saved to go toward the cost of your education? This dollar amount significantly affects how much debt you might have to take on absent any scholarships. If the dollar amount is closer to zero, I highly encourage you to consider starting to save and invest very early for the educational expenses of your children/future children to ensure they are in a better position before starting college. The same advice applies if you have some savings, moderate or substantial to cover your expenses. Why? I will ask you this, what goes up and seldom comes down? If you said cost of education, you would have picked one of the few correct answers. Now some of you science buffs were ready to lecture me about gravity and what goes up must come down. You know who you are! OK...Ok...back to it. We will include some savings to our table as below

Institution (College/University)	Option A	Option B	Option C
Total Cost	$85,000	$95,000	$55,000
Money Saved for Education Expenses	$1,000	$3,000	$2,000

You might have noticed by now that I did not include scholarships thus far. My reasoning is as follows: I am considering the worst case scenario planning. Scholarships might be one time, require certain criteria met to renew (such as grades or GPA) or students may not always qualify for scholarships or know the amount they could potentially qualify for. As previously mentioned, please develop this table to include as much information as you have available. This will help you make a much better informed decision.

5.1.1.6   HOW MUCH YOU WILL HAVE TO BORROW TO COVER COST

Time to tally…now I know some of you are thinking about the tally man, we are not counting bananas here but I'll give you a moment to run through the song. Tic tock, tic tock…done? Great!

Now let's tally our table above. We will subtract the total amount saved toward educational expenses from the total cost, to give us an estimate of how much will have to be borrowed for each scenario.

Institution (College/University)	Option A	Option B	Option C
Total Cost	$85,000	$95,000	$55,000
Money Saved for Education Expenses	$1,000	$3,000	$2,000
Estimated Loan Amount	$84,000	$92,000	$53,000

If your table is more complex than the one we are currently working on, here is what you do; add all non-refundable amounts of money that will go toward educational costs for the length of your studies (such as your savings, scholarships, federal aid, etc.), and subtract this from the total cost. If you end up with a positive number, that is an estimate of how much you will need in student loans. If your result is zero or negative, lucky you! You might just be one of a few students to potentially graduate without student loan debt.

5.1.1.7   AFFORDABLE COLLEGE ALTERNATIVE

Remember I previously mentioned to select at least two to three college options before. You need to ask yourself if you can find an alternative to the three options (A,B and C) analyzed so far, that will give you a good quality education in the same field of interest at a more affordable rate than all three (in this case, graduating with an estimated less than $53,000 in student loans per option C). Let us assume all these universities give you a good quality education with access to the same employment opportunities and wages. It makes financial sense to select option C in the absence of a more affordable alternative as explained above. You should take as many practical factors into consideration to lower the cost of education without compromising quality.

5.1.1.8   WORKING WHILE GOING TO SCHOOL

Generally, I would strongly recommend this option, especially if you can work and maintain good grades. Let us be clear about one thing here, this is by no means an easy option. Most days you will be as tired as a cow pulling a plow and those would be the good days but as painful and undesirable as it may seem, it is well worth it in the end. I can tell you that from personal experience. I worked throughout school, part time initially then full time and until today, I am glad I did because I took no student loans thanks to help from family, wages earned while working and scholarships. This option will likely not give you the greatest college experience given you will be at school mostly for classes and then straight off to work. However, it saved me from years of student loan debt payments – I am happy and you will be too!

5.1.1.9   POTENTIAL INCOME POST GRADUATION

It is critical to evaluate how much you can realistically earn after completing your degree. This and other financial obligations you have or will have will determine your ability to pay back any loans. Be conservative in estimating your future income. If you are considering post graduate studies, this is also very important in analyzing how much increase in earning potential your degree will bring. Note that increase wages due to an advance degree may not be significant immediately after completion. Some post graduate educational opportunities open up doors for you later on as you continue to gain experience in your field.

5.1.1.10 *CAN YOU PAY DEBT AND COMFORTABLY INVEST IN YOUR FUTURE?*

Currently you may just be thinking as far ahead as the length of time it would take to complete your education but you should look far beyond that. Granted, we can plan all we want and sometimes, life decides to take us a different path. However, at least you should plan well with the knowledge and realistic expectations you currently have. If your plans are not feasible on paper, it is hard to see how they will be feasible in real life. Now back to some of the things to consider for/in the future – will you

a)   Get married?
b)   Start a family?
c)   Relocate?
d)   Be responsible for a relative (aging parent, ailing sibling, etc.)?
e)   Buy a house?
f)   Buy a car?
g)   Have any other short, medium or long term financial commitments?

These give you an idea of the things you should be thinking of that will greatly affect your future cash flow. This is important because taking a student loan is usually a long term financial commitment to repay the debt and should be considered in tandem with all possible future expenses that will to lead you to take on more debt.

The age old advice of always paying yourself first still applies. So, you should subtract your savings from your anticipated future income before analyzing your ability to repay any loans. It is very important that when you estimate your future income, you should err on the side of caution and use a conservative (lower) income at the start of your career. As you gain more experience, raises will come along and you will likely get more money available to save/invest.

Each decision you make regarding debt affects your ability to take additional debt or save and invest. I recommend you minimize the amount of debt you take on but unfortunately most of us do not have the cash lying around to pay for a house or a car in full.

Here is an example of how current debt decisions affect your future; The Savvy family is in the market for a house. Their household income is about $60,000. Mr. and Mrs. Savvy had narrowed down their options to two houses at $130,000 and $160,000, and finally decided to go for the cheaper house. Assuming either loan has the same interest rate, down payment and term, the Savvy family will benefit from paying less interest on the loan, have a lower contractual mortgage payment relative to buying a $160,000 house. This allows them to have more money available to save, invest or make extra mortgage payments to principal. If in the future, the Savvy family needs a new vehicle, all things being equal, they would be in a financially better position to afford one because of their decision to opt for the $130,000 house earlier instead of the $160,000 house.

The example we just went through is simplified but still has a realistic lesson to be learned – minimize your debt and you will have more to save, invest or resolve future financial obligations.

5.1.1.11 MAXIMUM ACCEPTABLE PAY OFF TERM

Take a moment to ask yourself how many years you are willing to take to pay off your student loan. Write that number down somewhere. We will analyze that scenario soon with some numbers so we get a better understanding. By the way, the standard repayment period for federal student loans is 10 years. How does your number from earlier compare?

Visit www.studentaid.gov and use the repayment calculator to review repayment options, monthly payment amounts and estimate total interest paid on the loan. This calculator is used in the following example for a Texas family of three, with a total subsidized loan balance of $53,000 (from university C in our tables above) at 3.8% interest. The family's adjusted gross income is $90,000, married and filing joint tax returns. The standard repayment period of 10 years will require a $532 monthly repayment, resulting in a total estimated interest of over $10,000. You need to determine if you can afford to pay this amount for 10 years, considering other additional future financial obligations such as mortgage payments, car payments, child care costs, medical bills, etc. I should point out here that even though the loan taken was $53,000, because of the $10,000+ interest paid over a 10 year period with the standard repayment period option, the total cost exceeds $63,000! You do not have to take the full 10 years to repay your loan. There are other payment options available but in general, shorter terms require larger monthly payments and longer terms with lower monthly payments will cost you more in overall interest paid. Graduated payments are also offered but may eventually have monthly obligations that are much higher than the standard payment plan. Visit the site mentioned above and research possible payment options, weigh affordability with loan term and or overall interest paid and make an informed decision. There is a wealth of information at www.studentaid.gov and I recommend using it as a starting point in your research. Also research interest rates for the loan you are considering and use them in the calculator mentioned above.

5.1.1.12 *VOLATILITY IN YOUR FIELD/CAREER*

Your ability to pay back any loans you take are also dependent on the stability of the career path you select post graduation. Volatility in a field does not always mean you should not pursue that career path but it does mean you have to plan for it; when things are good, save and invest with consideration that when consistent work is not available, you can still continue to meet your financial obligations. I know you are currently thinking that if there is volatility in the future and you lose your job, you could always apply for a student loan payment deferment. True, but a deferment is just that…a deferment! You still have to continue paying the student loan after the deferment expires.

The aim is to get you to the point where you are debt free and part of that is making sure you take as little debt as possible or no debt at all. A steady career provides additional security that you will likely have consistent income available to be able to continuously make payments to any student loan balance you may have.

5.1.1.13 *ALTERNATE CAREER PATH*

Sometimes, we have more than one career path that we are equally passionate about. If you find yourself in this situation and have analyzed your primary option and the total cost of completing the degree is astronomical, by all means, consider your other passion. In order to do a proper analysis of both options, you need to consider both the likely debts you will accumulate versus the relative earning potential for each career. A higher earning potential gives you the ability to be able to pay off a relatively larger student loan.

I feel it is imperative I stress that just because your future career has high earning potential does not mean you should take any more loans than absolutely necessary.

Another perspective if I may, assume you have student loan debt and your monthly payment is $300, with an annual salary of $50,000 or about $24 an hour. You are single and live in Illinois with a 3.75% state income tax rate. Your actual take home hourly rate after your payroll tax deductions reduce from $24 to about $18. If you were to include other deductions for items such as medical, dental and vision insurance, retirement contributions, your net take home hourly wage decreases even further. A 10% contribution to your retirement account in addition to the above will drop your net hourly take home pay to $16 ($33,280 annually), down to two thirds of the initial $24 per hour ($50,000 per year).

Average monthly net take home: $33,280 / 12 = $2,773

Student loan: $300

Percentage of average monthly take home going toward student loan repayment:

$$= \frac{\$300}{\$2,773} x100\% \approx 11\%$$

In this case (even without considering insurance premiums), your loan payments will be about 11% of your average monthly take home. A direct calculation using your gross income $4,167 ($50,000/12) would have yielded about 7%.There are guidelines published for what the maximum percentage of your discretionary or disposable income should be used to pay off student loans but at the end of the day, they are only guidelines. You should decide what is acceptable to you, given your current and projected financial situation. Are you fine with 11% of your income for the next 10+ years going to repay a debt? Remember to always aim to minimize debt as much as possible!

5.1.1.14 *LOAN INTEREST RATE AND FEES*

As with any other loans, student loans also carry an interest rate and some fees. You should research each loan type you are seeking to ensure you are well informed of the associated interest rate and fees. Details of the rates and fees and/or different loan types will not be covered here as these are determined by the government and the most up-to-date information is available at https://studentaid.ed.gov/sa/, an office of the US Department of education. For those outside of the United States, refer to your respective Ministries or relevant governmental body handling these loans if available.

The interest rate charged on a student loan will directly impact your estimation of how much you are willing and capable of paying monthly and also how long it takes you to pay off the loan. Generally, federal loan interest rates for undergraduate studies carry lower interest rates compared to those for graduate studies and professionals.

Since we are on the subject of interest rates, we should examine two types of direct federal loans- subsidized and unsubsidized student loans.

a)   SUBSIDIZED STUDENT LOANS

Direct subsidized loans are available for undergraduate students based solely on need, which will be determined by the school you are attending or chose to attend. While you are still enrolled at least part time and up to six months after graduation, the interest that accrues during this period will be paid for by the government (Department of Education). Interest may also be paid for during periods of loan deferment. There are circumstances under which the government will cease to pay the interest and you become fully responsible for payments. Visit the student aid website mentioned above for additional information.

b)   UNSUBSIDIZED STUDENT LOANS

In contrast to subsidized loans, these are not granted based on need and are available to undergraduate and graduate students. However, you (the borrower) are responsible for paying any interest on the loan as specified in the loan agreement. The government does not subsidize any payments for any period of time. Your school also determines the amount you can borrow based on the total cost of attendance and any financial assistance you receive.

Graduate students and Professionals can also consider the Direct Plus federal student loans. Details and instructions are also available at the web address previously provided.

For interest payment that you are responsible for during your time in school up to and including the grace period, if these payments are not made, they will be added to the principal of your loan and you will then be required to pay it back with additional interest. The grace period is for the repayment of the loan principal balance only and not any interest accrued.

Just as I have mentioned before, be careful when you take out loans, be sure you are fully aware of the terms of the loan and you should only borrow what you need.

There are also private student loans available but I recommend you choose the federal aid option first. The government is not a for-profit institution unlike the bank and you are likely to get better loan benefits through the federal government such as subsidized interest payments or loan forgiveness programs just to name a few.

All the federal student loan types mentioned so far have an associated loan fee ranging from a little over 1% to over 4% for the Direct Plus loans. The fee amount is deducted from the loan amount for which you are approved. Interest rates vary from just over 3% to over 6%. Interest rates and fees are subject to change; refer to the Department of Education website for current rates.

5.1.2   CREDIT CARDS

There are many theories on how and when credit cards should be used, some state for emergencies only, others for select recurring purchases in order to build credit. In the end, we all need and use credit for different reasons and so we should tailor our credit card usage to meet our needs. The key in all of this is to ensure you do not carry a revolving balance on your account. I am sure you have heard many horror stories about people getting into significant credit card debt. While these are pertinent experiences to learn from, the key is to use any form of credit responsibly and you will be able to steer clear of making yourself the next horror financial story others read about on blogs.

In the United States, credit card interest rates are typically in the range of 13% to 23% APR, with some credit cards offering a 0% APR for an introductory period such as three, six or twelve months. APR stands for annual percentage rate, therefore a 20% APR is equivalent to a daily interest rate of 0.054795% (20%/365 days). To calculate your accrued interest, the credit issuer takes your daily balance and multiplies it by the daily interest rate until the end of your billing period. This next point is important, as long as you make your payments in full, no interest payments are required. If however you do carry a balance, there will be interest charged on any balance carried forward from any given billing cycle. As an example, you initially carried no balance, at the end of your January bill cycle your credit card bill is $750. You make a payment of $500 and carryover $250, you will not be charged any interest on the $500 paid but you will pay interest on the $250 balance carried forward in your February billing cycle.

5.1.2.1   *CREDIT CARD USAGE*

As long as you use credit responsibly, I believe credit cards should be used whenever needed. Emphasis on needed. Use your credit card with a debit card mentality; if you do not have the funds to pay off any purchase at the end of that billing cycle, avoid using your credit card. Since life is not ideal, there may be some emergency cases that arise where you may have to use your credit card and carry a balance but I urge you to consider this as a last resort. Consider picking up a gig or borrowing from family before this option. If you borrow from family or friends, be sure to pay them back on time or earlier, do not damage your relationships or become the person they avoid…you know who you are!

Credit cards offer better protection than debit cards in case of unauthorized purchases. This is a major reason why it is better to use your credit card for online purchases to provide an additional layer of protection in case your card information is compromised. Credit cards may also carry a host of other benefits such as travel insurance, rental car insurance, price protection guarantee, damage protection, etc. Refer to the details in the fine print that came along with your credit card to confirm what benefit(s) if any, are included.

The method I suggest to use below is not for everyone, if you keep your credit card in a block of ice in your freezer, this is not likely a method for you. Only use this method if you are disciplined enough to pay off your balance at the end of the month.

Credit cards today have all types of rewards to select from, cash back, airline miles, reward points to name a few. Some cards offer as much as 5% cash back on purchases in various categories such as groceries, gas, travel, home improvement and a base 1% on all other purchases. At some point, if you support a household, you will have to buy groceries, pay utility bills, shop at a home improvement store, buy gas for your vehicle (if you own one); these are all items you need and can pay for them with a credit card. Using your credit card in these instances will generate rewards points or cash back that you can accumulate and use for other purposes. At 5% cash back, a quarterly (3 month) grocery bill of $1,000 will yield $50 cash back reward. Again I insist this only works in your advantage if you pay off the balance at the end of each billing period. This cash back can be used to either supplement cost of other needs or applied towards a bill payment. You end up making a little money for responsibly using credit. In addition, this will also build up your credit history.

We talked about needs above and I pointed out specific examples of expenditures anyone would incur while running a home. You can also use this method to buy other things you want, as long as you budgeted for them and saved enough to cover the cost. This method only works in your advantage if you pay off the balance at the end of each billing period. You end up making a little money for responsibly using credit cards for expenditures you cannot avoid. Do not get carried away swiping your credit cards because of rewards as this is counterproductive and dangerous. You should still stick to your budget and aim to spend as little as possible while maximizing your savings and investments.

5.2 EXISTING DEBT

You may already be in debt and hoping to dig yourself out of that hole. If you are in debt, the first step to getting out is to stop spending and re-evaluate your needs and wants. We will cover some more common forms of debt such as credit card debt, mortgages and student loans. Most of the strategies outlined are applicable to getting rid of other types of debt. Interest rates on debt are a direct measure of what that debt is costing you. Higher interest rate debt means you are paying more in interest to the lender. Therefore, you should always strive to pay off debts with high interest rates faster than others.

5.2.1 CREDIT CARD DEBT

There is a significant disadvantage in carrying credit card debt because they tend to have one of the highest interest rates. Even with excellent credit, your interest rate will likely be in the double digits! If you constantly have a rolling credit card balance through different billing cycles, then it is time to admit to yourself that you are likely not using credit properly and living above your means. Whenever the phrase "living above your means" is uttered, we mostly think of someone living lavishly and splurging with money they do not have. In reality, you could be living above your means and still not live a life of luxury. Your "means" or source of income is what determines what your lifestyle should be. In any case, you should always strive to live below your means and invest as much as you can. Some steps to take to handle credit card debt are outlined next.

5.2.1.1 CREATE A BUDGET OR REVISE YOUR EXISTING BUDGET

You have realized that you have too much credit card debt; the next step should be to immediately stop making additional charges to your credit card(s) and prepare a budget or revisit your existing budget to make modifications. If you do not track all your expenses already, I suggest you start doing so. Refer to your credit and debit card statement history to track where you typically spend your money. This will help you eliminate expenditures that are not considered a need. We have previously discussed budgeting, if you need a refresher, refer to that chapter.

Your budget should include all your planned expenses and debt payments. Some or all of the additional dollars made available as a result of this budget evaluation or revision can be used to pay down credit card balance(s).

5.2.1.2 *MINIMIZE INTEREST PAYMENTS*

If you have more than one credit card with a running balance, you should pay off the card with the highest interest rate first. This should cut down on the overall interest you will have to pay. Also ensure to make more than the minimum payments for the other accounts as this will reduce interest paid, time to pay off balance and also help your credit score. You need to plan to aggressively pay down your balance to rid yourself of debt.

Example: If you have a $2,500 credit card balance at 20% APR with a minimum payment of the greater of interest plus 3% of principal balance owed or $15. It would take you 14 years to pay off the card balance and you would have paid over $2,700 in interest if you paid only the required minimum monthly amount. If you kept your payments at $75 fixed per month, it would take 4 years and cost almost $1,200 in interest payments. At $100 a month fixed, it would take about 2 years and 9 months and just under $800 in interest payments. The lesson here is to always pay more than the required minimum payments.

Another option to help pay down credit card debt is to transfer all your credit card balance to a card that offers 0% APR for balance transfers for a certain time period. Select a card with the longest available interest-free period and terms that favor your particular situation. Do not, charge additional expenses to this card or any other credit card you own which will result in a higher balance transfer.

Using the example above with a $2,500 balance transferred to a card offering 0% interest for 24 months and 20% thereafter. Balance after the 2 year 0% interest period is $ 700 ($2,500 - $75x24) with a $75/month fixed payment. It would take an additional 11 months at $75/month to pay down the remaining $700 at 20% (total interest is less than $70). This is will be paid off about a year earlier and over $1,100 less in interest payments relative to the option without a balance transfer.

If you could pay $100/month, you will be left only with a balance of $100 after 24 months with the same balance transfer card terms. Your 25th month payment will be about $102, with a total interest paid below $2. This option will shave off 12 years of payment relative to making the minimum required payment at 20% APR.

If you do not have good enough credit to qualify for a 0% balance transfer card, call your credit card company and request an interest rate reduction. You can explain that you are willing to meet your obligations but payments have become difficult for you to afford. There is no guarantee that this will result in your rate being decreased but you have nothing to lose. Worst case scenario, the answer is a no. They will not send someone to your home to give you a cautionary beating just in case you think of missing a future payment!

5.2.1.3   *INCREASE INCOME OR DECREASE COST*

Learn to use credit more responsibly. If your budget contains only needs and you still end up needing to use credit to make ends meet, then you may want to consider other options such as requesting for a raise at work (the reason should be work performance related, not "my bills are too high"), find a second/part time job, finding a better paying full time job, discuss possibility of a non working spouse going back to work fulltime or part time. See the budgeting section for some ideas on how to decrease cost of needs. If your rent and/or cost of living in your area are too high, you may have to ultimately consider moving to a cheaper area with similar opportunities.

5.2.2   STUDENT LOAN DEBT

Skyrocketing cost of education means that more college graduates will have student loan debt to pay off. Some of the strategies already outlined also apply to student loan debt. You should strive to pay off the highest interest rate loans first. Budget re-evaluation should also be undertaken and increase income/decrease cost should also be incorporated in your plans. There are a few things to note about federal student loan debt that we will cover. Refer to the department of education for additional payment options or details on paying off student loans at www.studentaid.gov .

5.2.3   FEDERAL STUDENT LOAN CONSOLIDATION

Federal student loan consolidation does not decrease the interest paid on the outstanding loan balance. The interest rate of the consolidated loan is the weighted average of interest rates for all the individual loans. While consolidating your loans will not help lower your interest rate, it can help simplify how you manage your payments. Instead of multiple payments being made monthly to individual loans, you will only have a single payment.

5.2.4   FEDERAL STUDENT LOAN DEFERMENT

During a deferment period, the repayment of your principal and interest are delayed. The federal government may pay the interest on your loan during this period depending on the loan type. No interest payments will be made on unsubsidized and PLUS loans. For interest payments that are your responsibility and not paid during a deferment, the interest owed will be added to your principal balance, leading to even higher payments after the deferment period. Deferring your loan does not make it go away. It may actually end up costing you more!

5.2.5   FEDERAL STUDENT LOAN FORBEARANCE

During forbearance, your payments can be halted or reduced for up to 12 months. Do not celebrate yet. Interest will continue to accrue on all loan types in forbearance. You can elect to pay this interest during the forbearance period or it will be added to your principal.

The key to paying off any loan faster is to cut down the interest rate or pay off the principal faster. Always remember, when investing, time is your friend, when in debt, time is your foe! In our previous discussion on things to consider before taking on debt, we examined payoff time. This might be a good time to review what was covered. Examine your finances carefully before selecting a length of payment that will fit within your budget while ensuring you pay down the principal as fast as possible. As with any debt, you should make additional payments to the principal to decrease total interest paid and length of time to pay off.

5.2.6   MORTGAGE

See the section on refinance in the chapter on mortgages.

If your mortgage becomes too expensive for you, I would also recommend you talk to your lender as early as possible to figure out your options. Evaluate these carefully before making a decision on how to proceed.

Selling your house is another option to consider if you find you cannot afford payments anymore and refinancing is not possible. You should ensure that you are not upside-down on your mortgage (owe more than the house is worth) before selling, else you will still be in debt if you sell. If home ownership still appeals to you after selling, you can buy a more affordable house afterwards and be sure to plan properly this time around.

If you do not want to sell, you can also consider renting out your home to tenants to cover your mortgage payments. Note that this option also comes with a lot of responsibility and liability. You should check the local landlord laws and talk to an expert or attorney to ensure you have a valid lease agreement and requisite insurance coverage.

6 PLANNING FOR RETIREMENT

We go through life in different stages and for those who are lucky to stay alive through their golden years, the time to retire will eventually come. It is important to start preparing for this stage in life as early as you can. I have encountered various iterations of procrastination from "I am still young and I have enough time to start later" to "I'll cross that bridge when I get there". In truth, the earlier you start building the bridge of securing an income source in retirement, the easier the transition is likely to be. It is important to set a realistic goal as to how much money you should accumulate prior to retiring. This estimate should be made based on your projected expenses and style or standard of living in retirement. In order to be accurate, you need a magic crystal ball to see in the future. In the absence of that, be conservative in estimating expenses and plan to save more money than your calculations state you may require, you would be better off with an excess later on, instead of a shortage.

6.1 TIME VALUE OF MONEY (TVM)

Before we proceed, we should discuss the time value of money. This is the concept that if money can earn interest, a fixed amount of money is worth more today (because it can be invested for potential profit and an increase in overall value) relative to the same amount in the future. A simple example, if $500 can earn 10% interest in 1 year, receiving $500 today is more valuable than $500 in one year because if you invest the $500 you receive today, after one year, at 10%, you will have $550.

The TVM is also affected by Inflation; the increase in prices of goods and services and the decrease in the purchasing power of money. As a simple example, if annual inflation rate is at say 2%, if an item costs $100 this year, it would cost $102 to buy the same item next year.

It is important to understand these simple but important concepts because they greatly affect how to estimate cost of living when you retire and how much/soon you should start contributing. Based on these two concepts, TVM recommends you start contributing to an investment account as soon as possible to maximize gains, inflation cautions you to estimate your retirement costs carefully and conservatively in order to make a proper plan of action.

6.2 RETIREMENT INVESTMENT OPTIONS:

There are certain investments options specifically tailored for retirement financial planning that may provide some tax benefits but you should not be limited to these. When you maximize the use of these tax advantaged options, consider other investment options that will help you continuously grow wealth. We shall explore some of the more common tax advantaged retirement plans next.

6.2.1   EMPLOYER SPONSORED 401K PLAN

In the United States, 401K plans are tax advantaged plans that allow employees to contribute money to invest for retirement in a group of securities selected by the employer. There are two types of 401K plans, the Traditional and Roth 401k plans. An employer may elect to match the employee contribution to their retirement account up to a certain limit. Consult with your employer to find out what these limits are.

A.   TRADITIONAL 401K

In a traditional 401K plan, the employee contribution and employer match (if any) are made on a pretax basis. Income taxes will be charged only when the employee makes withdrawals (in retirement). A necessary clarification here is that pretax refers only to federal taxes. Medicare, social security and state taxes are calculated based on gross income.

B.   ROTH 401K

In a Roth 401K plan, employee contributions are made after taxes have been paid. When the employee makes withdrawals in retirement, no additional taxes will be levied. Important to note here that any company match is pretax and income taxes will be charged when withdrawals are made.

The maximum contribution you can make to a traditional 401K, Roth 401K or a combination of both for 2017 is $18,000 (this does not include the company match). For those of us over the age of 50, there is an additional catch-up contribution of up to $6,000 that can be made to your 401K accounts. Check the Internal Revenue Service website for updated contribution limits.

Employer matches may be offered as a single or tiered match. As an example an employer may offer to match 100% of employee contributions up to 4% of their gross annual income or offer to match the employee contribution 100% for the first 3% and 50% for the next two percent. Both of these offer a maximum match of 4% but why are they different? In the first case, an employee only has to contribute 4% to receive the maximum employer match of 4%. In the second case, for the employee to receive the full match, a 5% contribution has to be made (100% match on the first 3% plus 50% for next 2%; 50% of 2% is 1%). While I always recommend contributing the maximum or at least strive to max out your retirement contributions, it is important to understand the difference in these two scenarios to ensure that you are receiving at least all the company match offered. No need letting free money get away, right?

Another point to also clarify with your employer is how the match is offered. The match may be offered as fixed payments over 12 months contingent on your contributions to retirement from every single paycheck. In other words, if you reach your contribution limit before the end of the year, you may likely not get the full match offered by your employer because no additional contributions were made by you after reaching your maximum and therefore no matching contributions are paid by your employer. To avoid this, calculate what percentage of your salary needs to be deducted for retirement savings. If you get a raise at some point in the year, you need to redo this calculation.

The employer match is not always immediately 100% guaranteed to the employee. Some employers elect to use a vesting schedule. What this implies is that the employer will provide the match to your account as agreed, but they will set a timeline for when that match will become 100% yours. A sample 5-year vesting schedule for an employee match could be as follows: 10% after 1 year, 60% after 3 years and 100% after 5 years. This means if you quit the company after 3 years, you will only get 60% of the entire employer matching contributions made up to your separation date. You will still receive the full amount of your contributions.

6.2.2   INDIVIDUAL RETIREMENT ACCOUNT (IRA)

The IRA is also a tax advantaged plan similar to the 401K. However, the major difference relative to the 401K is that the plan is not held by an employer, so you do not have to work for a particular company to be eligible to make contributions. IRA maximum contributions are limited to the lesser of $5,500 increased to $6,500 if over age 50 or your taxable income. IRAs also offer a wider selection of investment options as opposed to 401K plans which only have a few hand-picked funds in their plan.

A.   TRADITIONAL IRA

Contributions to Traditional IRA accounts may be tax deductable if you are single or married filing jointly and do not have any employer sponsored retirement plan. If you or your spouse (or both) have an employer sponsored retirement plan, your contribution may be tax deductable if you meet certain income requirements. Refer to the IRS for the most up to date limits for eligibility for tax deductions.

Anyone aged 70 ½ or younger is eligible to regularly contribute to a Traditional IRA up to the maximum amount allowed as long as their taxable income is at least the dollar amount of their contributions.

B.   ROTH IRA

Contributions to a Roth IRA are made with after tax dollars. Withdrawals in retirement are tax free. There are no age limitations for Roth IRA contributions, however, there are income limitations which phase out contribution amounts or make you ineligible to participate in a Roth IRA plan. Per the IRS, you can contribute to a Roth IRA for 2017 if you had taxable income and your modified adjusted gross income (AGI) is:

- Less than $186,000 for married filing jointly or qualifying widow/widower up to the limit.
- $186,000 but $196,000 or less for married filing jointly or qualifying widow/widower at a reduced amount.
- Less than $118,000 for single, head of household or married filing separately and did not live with your spouse at any time during the year up to the limit.

- $118,000 but less than $133,000 for single, head of household or married filing separately and did not live with your spouse at any time during the year at a reduced amount.
- Less than $10,000 for married filing separately if you lived with your spouse at any time during the year at a reduced amount.

Check with the Internal Revenue Service for the updated income limitations and conditions for contributing to a Roth IRA or tax deductions for Traditional IRAs.

EXAMPLES:

a.   If Jane, 24 years old, worked part time and has an annual taxable income of $4,500, she can only contribute a maximum of $4,500 to her IRA (taxable income is less than IRS maximum contribution rate of $5,500).

b.   Jill, 27 years old, has an annual taxable income of $50,000. Jill can contribute the IRS maximum of $5,500 to her IRA.

Even though regular contributions to a traditional IRA are limited to age 70 ½ or less, those over this age can still rollover funds into any IRA, Roth or Traditional. There are also tables published by the IRS stating limits for taking deductions for contributions to Traditional IRA accounts for those with and without a workplace 401K plan. Refer to the IRS website for the most up to date tables.

There are tax advantaged retirement plans available for the self-employed individuals, similar to those of employees. There is a one participant or solo-401K plan for the self employed with Roth and Traditional options, a maximum contribution of $18,000 plus an additional $6,000 for those over the age of 50. In addition, you can contribute up to 25% of your net self-employment earnings into the account up to a maximum of $54,000. All these limits are based on

IRS data for 2017. Refer to the IRS for additional information on the types of retirement plans available to the self-employed.

6.3 COST OF WAITING

In order to better prepare for retirement, we need to plan appropriately and start making contributions towards our retirement investments. Avoid procrastination and start as early as possible because there is a cost associated with waiting. In this case a missed opportunity. Recall we talked about the time value of money at the beginning of this chapter; a fixed amount of money is worth more today (because it can be invested for potential profit and an increase in overall value) relative to the same amount in the future.

Example:

Frank and Spencer are both 22 years old. Frank contributes $4,800 annually to his retirement account while Spencer waits 10 years to start making the same contribution amount. They both plan to retire at 65 years old. Assuming they get the same average annual rate of return of 6%, at 65, Frank will have about $900,000 available in his account while Spencer will have about $467,000. Note that the difference in the amount contributed by Frank is greater by $48,000 ($4,800/yr multiplied by 10 years). However, because of the additional time Frank has to invest, compounding interest works in his favor with $433,000 extra relative to Spencer. Spencer's cost of starting late relative to interest accrued is $385,000 ($443,000 minus $48,000)

To match the amount Frank has in his retirement account at 65, Spencer would have to make constant annual contributions of about $9,250 (almost double Frank's rate). Spencer's cost of waiting relative to amount contributed is $4,450 annually ($9,250 -$4,800) or $146,850 ($4,450/yr multiplied by 33 years) over the life of the investment.

When it comes to personal finance, you should generally adopt the motto of spending as little as possible and ensuring you invest in your future as much as possible. Sometimes investing in your future will require you to spend. Always focus your analysis on the bigger picture and the potential reward, to ensure your path forward is the best possible. Based on what we have covered together in this book, by now you see that there is no isolated financial decision. Each time you have expenditure, there is a missed opportunity to save and invest.